Fear of Abandonment

Fear of Abandonment

How To Heal Your Fear of Abandonment

Oliver JR Cooper

Also By Oliver JR Cooper

A Dialogue With The Heart – Part One: A
Collection Of Poems And Dialogues From The
Heart

Trapped Emotions – How Are They
Affecting Your Life?

Childhood – Is Your Childhood
Sabotaging Your Life?

A Dialogue With The Heart – Part Two: A
Collection Of Poems And Dialogues From The
Heart

Toxic Shame – Is It Defining Your Life?

Abandonment – Is The Fear Of Abandonment
Controlling Your Life?

Child Abuse – Were You Abused As A Child?

A Dialogue With The Spirit – A Collection Of
Poems And Dialogues To Help You Grieve The
Loss Of A Loved One

Trapped Grief – Is Trapped Grief Sabotaging
Your Life?

Why Does He Behave That Way? Why Do I Behave This Way?

Boundaries – Are You Boundaryless?

Inner Child – Is Your Inner Child Controlling Your Life?

Childhood Trauma – Is Childhood Trauma Defining Your Life?

People Pleasing – Is Your Need To Please Others Sabotaging Your Life?

Loyalty – Is Your Need To Be Loyal Sabotaging Your Life?

Trauma – Is Trauma Sabotaging Your Life?

How-To Guides

Inner Child – How To Heal Your Inner Child

Self-Awareness – How To Develop Self-Awareness

Purpose – How To Find Your Purpose

Anxiety – How To Deal With Your Anxiety

Breakups – How To Get Over A Breakup

Note to Readers

That which is contained within this book is based upon my own experiences, research, and views up until the point of publication. It is not to be taken as the truth or the only viable viewpoint. It is not intended to diagnose or cure any disease.

This book is dedicated to Ben Ralston. Thank you deeply for your guidance and support.

Fear of Abandonment – How To Heal Your Fear of Abandonment

ISBN: 9798678660794

For information, please contact:

www.oliverjrcooper.co.uk

Contents

Introduction

There are numerous fears that you can have that won't have much of an impact on your life, and there are other fears that will. When it comes to the type of fears that are unlikely to have much of an impact, examples could be a fear of snakes, heights or flying.

Of course, if you were to come across a snake, go to the top of a building or get on a plane, you might suffer, but these are things that you won't necessarily have to experience on a regular basis. When it comes to the fears that are likely to have a big effect on your life, it could relate to the fear of open spaces or being abandoned.

No matter where you live, you are likely to come across open spaces from time to time. When this happens, you could experience a fair amount of discomfort.

Still, this doesn't mean that you will spend a lot of time worrying about being in an open space. Yet when it comes to the fear of being abandoned, this can be a fear that occupies a lot of your attention.

Regardless of whether, or not, you are in the company of another person, this can be something that is on your mind. This fear can cause so much havoc, in fact, that it is more or less impossible for you to experience inner peace and to relax.

If you have been able to detach from this experience and to think about how long your life has been this way, you may have found that it has been this way for as long as you can remember. In this case, it won't be a fear that has only just started to cause you problems; it will be a fear that has been making it difficult for you to function for a very long time.

For most of your life, you may have believed that this was just how life was and that there was absolutely nothing that you could do about it. Fortunately, you will have been able to get to the point where you have been able to realise that this isn't the case.

Somehow, your mind will have been opened up to the truth that there is another way for you to experience life. Thanks to this, you will have decided to do something about what is taking place.

So while you will have suffered and are no doubt still experiencing a lot of pain, you will have been able to step back and to no longer be completely caught up in what has been going on previously. This is the first step to moving forward. If you were not able to become aware of what is going on, you would continue to experience life in the same way.

Therefore, while experiencing this awareness won't transform your life, it will allow you to do what you need to do to transform it. With this in mind, take the time to congratulate yourself on getting to this point on your healing journey.

Yes, there is still a long way for you to go and a lot of healing work that needs to be undertaken, but you have also come a long way to get to this stage. And I believe that no matter what your life is like at this point in time, if you commit to this path and don't give up, you will be able to gradually experience life differently.

If you expect too much too soon you can end up suffering unnecessarily, and this is why, I believe, at this stage you need to have a realistic outlook. I believe that you have what it takes to move through this fear so that it no longer controls you. But please be patient.

Although part of you may doubt that you have what it takes, part of you believes that you have what it takes which is why you are reading this book right now. This part of you, the part that knows that you are far more than what you fear, will grow as time goes by.

One way to see this part of you would be to say that it is your essence. It may have largely been covered up for many, many years, yet regardless of how many years pass, it won't go away.

Now is the time for you to take the next step in your healing journey and to allow this part of you to get even stronger. You have suffered for long enough and the time is now right for you to experience life differently.

With all that said, I will now endeavour to supply you with everything that you need to slowly transform your life. It will then be down to you to apply what I suggest, so that you can actually transform your life.

There may be times when you feel tired and exhausted and wonder if you have what it takes to move forward or to go further; given what you have been through, this is not surprising. After a while, you should soon get back on your feet and be ready to continue.

Do your best not to get too attached to these experiences and to let whatever goes on to pass you by. As the saying goes, 'what you resist persists' so keep this in mind when you are in a place of resistance.

Let's Begin.

The Symptoms

Irrespective of whether you are at the beginning of your life or have been on this planet for a little while, there are likely to be a number of ways in which your fear of abandonment has impacted your life. What you may find is that for as long as you can remember, you have had a strong need to please other people.

Putting other people's needs first and yours second or even overlooking your own needs will be the norm. But, even though this will have had a negative effect on your life, it could be normal for other people to describe you as 'selfless'.

Self-Neglect

Therefore, while you will have been neglecting yourself, it will have been seen as something positive to a lot of people. If this wasn't the case, and it was perfectly clear that you were neglecting yourself, you may have realised a long time ago that something wasn't right.

Still, this doesn't mean that every part of you has felt comfortable living in this way. But due to how fearful you have been, it wouldn't have been possible for you to actually listen to the discomfort that was inside you.

Split-Off

If you had listened to how you felt, you may have ended up getting really angry about what was going on. This anger would have been there to tell you that you were going against yourself.

The trouble is that due to what you feared would have happened if you asserted your own needs, you would have had to push this anger out of your awareness. This would have caused you to continue to ignore yourself, yet it would have been seen as being far better than the alternative.

Depressed

By ignoring this part of you, you may find that you have had the tendency to feel down, lack energy and be passive. This can be seen as a perfectly normal reaction to going against who you are.

It wouldn't be right to say that repressed anger will be the only reason why you often feel down, though. What can also play a part is that your life will be a reflection of your need to meet other people's needs as opposed to your own needs - not living your truth will make it hard for you to feel motivated and alive.

One Area

Maybe you are in a relationship with someone who is not a good match for you but who stops the fear that you have from coming to the surface. This relationship won't be fulfilling yet it will have filled the hole that is inside you, albeit temporarily.

It could be even worse, however, as you could be with someone who is extremely controlling. Deep down, this person may know that they can treat you badly as you are not going to leave them.

Previous Relationships

If you are single, you may find that every person that you have had a relationship with hasn't been a good match for you. Each time, only one part of your being may have been on board with the person that you were with.

This would have been the part of you that was concerned with your survival, with other parts of you being overlooked. In other words, your heart and even your intellect wouldn't have been involved.

The Only Option

At the same time, this is not to say that your intellect wouldn't have said that you were making the right decision. As it was a case of either being alone and suffering or being with someone else and not alone, going with someone may have been seen as the logical thing to do.

Due to what you fear, it may have been incredibly difficult for you to leave a relationship even if it·wasn't working. What you may have done is found someone else before you ended the previous relationship.

A Safety Net

This might not have been something that you wanted to do, but it may have been seen as the only solution to keeping your fear at bay. There may have even been times when you were in a relationship with more than two people at the same time.

That way, if one person left you, you would still have someone else there to stop your emotions and thoughts from getting out of control. And when you are with someone, you might need to spend a lot of time with them and to practically always talk to them over the phone or by sending messages.

Another Part

If you don't hear back from someone more or less straight away when you are in a relationship, it might not be long until you start to get anxious. Your mind could be filled with 'negative' thoughts and scenarios and certain feelings may start to arise.

This could be something that has happened previously even if there is nothing going on in the outside world that would suggest that your partner is going to pull away. What this fear may have done is caused your partner to pull away, thereby causing you to feel even worse.

Pulling Away

You may also see that you have left at least one relationship or stopped talking to someone out of your need to avoid being abandoned. Part of you may have believed that it was inevitable, so it was better for you to leave someone else than for them to leave you.

If this has taken place, the other person may have struggled to understand what happened. For a time, you may have even wondered why you did it, but it might not have been long until you found someone else or went with the person who you had already previously lined up.

Boundaries

There may have been times when you went along with things that you didn't want to do. This may often happen in other areas of your life. Instead of saying no, you would have said yes and there may have been times when you have said no when you wanted to say yes.

Once again, standing your ground and doing what was right would have felt like too much of a risk. Sure you would have compromised yourself, but it would have been seen as being better than the alternative.

Wearing a Mask

Perhaps you are someone who has typically come across as happy and easy-going, you might even be a bit of a chameleon, with this being a way for you to try to be sure that you don't upset or displease anyone. This is going to make it difficult for you to be authentic and to allow people to get close to the real you.

Ultimately, speaking your truth will have been a challenge and this may mean that you often have throat problems. What you have been unable to say will then have built up in your throat and other areas of your being.

Protection

Hiding your true self – your real needs and feelings - and putting on an act, will be seen as a way for you to try to stop people from leaving you. The reason that you will believe that you have to hide yourself in order to keep people around is because you will most likely believe that you are worthless.

As far as you are concerned, then, there will be something inherently wrong with who you are, which is why you need to do everything that you can to hide yourself. Being who other people want you to be, and who you think they want you to be, will be how this takes place.

Keeping a Distance

The irony here is even though you feel the need to always be in a relationship, it might not be possible for you to truly let anyone get close to you. Real intimacy is then not going to be something that you are able to experience.

Opening yourself up to someone is not going to be your priority; what will be your priority is just having someone there to settle you down. What could also play a part here is that you might also have a weaker fear of being smothered.

Another Consequence

Something else you may find is that when you are not in the company of a friend or partner, it is as though they don't exist. Not being able to realise that this is not the case will play a part in why you find it hard to feel emotionally settled in your own company.

In the world of psychology, this is something that is known as a lack of object permanence (or object constancy, depending on what source you read). If you were not neglected during your early years and were able to develop this cognitive ability, you would be able to maintain a connection with the people in your life, to realise that they still exist even when you can't see them and are not nearby, and this would make it a lot easier for your mind and your emotions to settle down when you are by yourself.

All About The Mind

What most of the above examples illustrate is that you have a fear of being abandoned and, along with this; you carry the belief that you have no value. Based on this, it can seem as though you have an irrational fear that you need to let go of and a belief that you need to change.

This will mean that you need to change what is taking place up top, in your mind, and then your life will be different. This might be something that you can accept or you may sense that there is far more to it.

Two Parts

If you do sense that there is more to it, it is likely to be a sign that you intuitively realise that it is not all about the mind. For some reason, you will know that it is also about what is taking place at a deeper level, with this relating to what is taking place in your body.

It is true that your thoughts can create how you feel but it can also work the other way around. Ergo, what is taking place in your body can cause what is taking place up top, and this is why it is not all about the mind.

It's Not All About The Mind

So much of the information out there, when it comes to self-development and even healing, focuses on the part that the mind plays. The mind plays a big part in how you experience life; there is no doubt about it.

Nonetheless, to focus purely on this part of your being and to overlook the part that your body is playing would be a massive oversight. You might only get so far by taking this route, and you may have already taken this route, only to find that it didn't allow you to move forward.

A Short-Term Solution

Focusing on your mind and playing around with your thoughts may have allowed you to experience life differently for a short while, but it might not have been long until you returned to how you were previously. If this is so, it might be even harder for you to handle what is going on.

Through having a taste of how different life can be, going back to how things were is naturally going to be tough. For a while, you may have come to the conclusion that there is nothing that you can do to change your life.

More to It

If it was all about your mind, changing what is going on up top would resolve this challenge. Changing the thoughts and beliefs that you have, along with your behaviour, would allow you to transform your life.

So why is your body important? The reason why your body is important here is because this part of you could be carrying the trauma of being abandoned, not once, but hundreds of times.

A More Accurate Description

What this means, then, is that not only do you have a fear of being abandoned; but you also carry the pain of being abandoned. Maybe this is something that you are already aware of.

Therefore, to say that you just have a fear of being abandoned is not the complete truth. If anything, the reason that you have a fear of being abandoned is due to the fact that you have already been abandoned so many times and part of you will fear coming into contact again with the deep pain that is inside you.

The Past Is Present

Part of you is then stuck in the past even though the past is in the past. To this part of you, it won't matter how many years pass or what you tell this part of you as it won't be able to be present.

There is a chance that what is going on for you as an adult is the result of what took place during your early years. During this time, your whole being may have been traumatised on a regular basis.

The Cause

Note: it is not essential for you to read this chapter. So if reading it would make things worse, please skip this chapter.

So practically from the moment that you were born, you may have been neglected by your caregiver/s. To be left at this stage of your life would have overwhelmed your whole system, and the only way for you to handle what was going on would have most likely been for you to disconnect from your body and to shut down.

The reason for this at this young age is that you wouldn't have had the ability to regulate your emotions. Whenever you were left, the intensity of the pain would have caused you to feel as though your life was going to end.

A Build Up

The love and care that you needed wouldn't have been provided, preventing you from developing in the right way. This would have caused your being to be loaded up with pain and it would have stopped your brain from developing in the right way.

If the right care had been provided and you were not left for such long periods of time, it would have most likely allowed your brain to develop in the right way. This would have allowed you to develop the ability to regulate your own emotions.

The Centre of the Universe

At this stage of your life you would have been egocentric; causing you to take what was going on personally. It was then not that you were left because of what was going on for your caregiver/s, it was because you were worthless.

17

Being left would have most likely flooded your system with shame as the interpersonal bridge between you and your caregiver/s was unable to develop. It would have been as though you had been cast aside and ostracised.

The Past repeats itself

Your caregiver/s may have been emotionally shut down, thereby allowing them to neglect you without thinking anything of it. Maybe they were also neglected at the beginning of their life.

For whatever reason they won't have healed what took place and this was why they passed on what they experienced. This could be something that goes back many, many generations.

The Seeds Were Sown

These early experiences would then have stopped you from being able to develop a strong sense of self, the ability to soothe yourself and caused you to believe that you were inherently flawed, amongst other things. A time in your life that should have built you up and prepared you for the world would have done the opposite.

Without strong foundations, it is to be expected that you would grow up to be someone who is emotionally stunted and is therefore emotionally dependent on others. If you had received the right care, you would probably be a very different person.

Self-Compassion

So if you have been hard on yourself over the years and believed that there is something inherently wrong with you, you will be able to at least consider the fact that this is not the case. You have simply done your best to cope with the destructive effects that early neglect had on your being.

Other people may have judged how you have behaved, yet if they had gone through what you have, they would probably be doing the same thing. Please keep this in mind if ever other people put you down or if part of you puts you down.

Before This Point

Having said this, you may have been left from the moment you were born. What this could show is that your birth was traumatic and you had to be taken away from your mother and put in an incubator.

As a small baby, you wouldn't have known what was going on and this would have been a lot for you to tolerate. What took place as time went by would then have been a continuation of what you experienced as soon as you entered the world.

A Lot to Handle

If one of your family members or friends has just had a baby, it might be possible for you to get an idea of how painful this time in your life must have been. Like this baby, you would have been totally powerless - there was absolutely nothing that you could have done.

That was in the past, though, and this is the present, and now you can do something about what is taking place for you. You are no longer a baby or even a child, but the child and baby that you once were still live inside you.

The Next Step

You might be able to relate to all of this or only some of it, but irrespective of this, you will want to find out about what it is that you can do to change your life. So, let's take a look at what you can do to gradually transform your life.

The First Part

The First part

External support

As I wrote in the previous chapter, the child that you once were now exists inside you. Or to be more precise, there are many child selves that are now inside you, meaning that you have many inner children.

This might be something that you can resonate with; alternatively, it could be something that sounds strange and a bit airy fairy. Ultimately, I don't think it matters if you can relate to this or not.

Another Angle

The reason for this is that even If you can't connect to this idea, what you will most likely find is that there are times when you regress. In fact, you may find that this is something that happens on a regular basis.

When this takes place, you could feel like a small child. If you can relate to the inner child way of looking at this then this will be a time when you have merged with a child self and if you can't, it will just be a time when you have regressed to an earlier stage in your life.

All at Sea

What will be crystal clear at this stage is that when you go from feeling like an adult to feeling like a child, you are not going to feel strong and centred. Your adult self will go offline and you will feel like a fearful, powerless, needy and incapable child.

What is going in will be too much for you to handle and this is going to mean that it is not going to be possible for you to be there for the child that is inside you. For you to be there for this part of you, you

25

will need to develop a strong adult self; a self that will be strong enough to be there for your child self.

External Support

If you had a strong adult self and a strong emotional core to go with it, and didn't just merely play the role of an adult at certain times and feel very weak under the role, you would be able to be there for this part of you and to allow it to express what it was unable to express all those years ago. Fortunately, this is something that you can gradually develop with the right support.

One way for you to connect to what I'm talking about would be to imagine that a building is nearly falling down and with the help of scaffolding; it is more secure. With this scaffolding erected, the necessary work will be able to go ahead so that the building can stay in place without external support.

Holding the Space

For instance, a therapist, or a healer, will provide the external support that you need to face what is taking place inside you as opposed to running away from it. This doesn't mean that you will have a few sessions and you will be on your way, or that you will have to go really deep straight away.

The important thing will be for you to listen to yourself and to move at a rate that feels comfortable for you. You may find that it takes a little while for you to trust the person enough to be able to open up to them.

Listen To Yourself

This is not to say that you should force yourself to trust them though, as they might not be the right person for you. If you get a sense that something isn't right, it might be best for you to look for someone else, and you may find that you feel more comfortable working with a man than a woman or vice versa.

Having said that, if you find that you don't feel comfortable with anyone, it could show that part of you is trying to avoid doing this work. To this part of you, opening up could be seen as something that is far too much of a risk.

Keep Going

This is something that you can acknowledge; there is no need for you to judge yourself if this is taking place. Once you are able to find someone who you feel comfortable with, you will be able to explore what is going on for you.

The safe container that a therapist or a healer will provide will allow you to go where you wouldn't go by yourself. Not only will you be able to work through how you feel, but you will also be able to reveal your true self to this person.

Unconditional Positive Regard

As you believe that there is something wrong with who you are, you won't have felt safe enough to reveal your true self – or this will have been something that has rarely taken place. Naturally, this will have stopped other people from being able to see the real you and to let you know that there is nothing wrong with you.

27

When you are in the presence of a therapist, or healer, however, you will be able to gradually reveal who you are and through receiving their positive feedback, you can start to understand, at a deeper level, that you have no need to hide yourself. What this comes down to, is that the toxic shame that you are likely to be carrying can only exist in hiding; it has to be brought into the light to dissipate.

Building a Bridge

The connection that you were unable to build with your caregiver/s during your early years, your connection to humanity, will then develop as an adult. The type of feedback that this person will show you won't be something that the average person can provide for you and it certainly won't be something that you can provide for yourself.

If you believe that needing this type of assistance means that you are weak or even incapable, it will be essential for you to remember that you are an interdependent human being – you are not your own island. Taking into account the position that you are currently in – currently, as this is just a stage - reaching out for support is the most sensible action you could take.

Inner Strength

Suffering in silence and trying to do everything by yourself is not going to benefit you. This is something that part of you understands, hence, why you have reached out for support by investing in this book.

What you are doing now takes courage. As long as you keep going and do what is necessary, your life will change. It may be clear at this point that it takes energy to do this work and this is why the more energy you have the better.

The Second Part

The Second Part

Energy

As energy is needed for most things to happen, it is not exactly a surprise that healing work is any different. Even so, you may find that you don't have much energy.

There can be at least two reasons as to why this is the case. To begin with, the trauma that you are carrying can take a lot out of you. Following this, you might be living in a way that undermines you.

The First Part

When it comes to the trauma that you are carrying, there will be what you can do to clear this out. As you work through the layers that are being held inside you, you will create more room for the energy to flow.

Your whole being can start to work better as this progresses, meaning your body and brain can function in a way that is less restricted. While you are carrying so much trauma this is going to be a lot harder.

The Second Part

If you are not getting enough sleep, exercising enough or eating the right foods this is going to sap your energy. For you to function fully, you will probably need to get each of these areas of your life in order.

You may find that you need to sleep for about 7 or 8 hours and that going to bed at the same time and waking up at the same time helps. Having a sleeping routine will give your life structure and, if you find it hard to feel settled, this will be a massive benefit.

The Importance of Structure

In the same way that a therapist or a healer will provide you with the external support that you need while you build up your inner support, having external structure will serve a similar purpose. This external structure will be there to give you a helping hand until you have built yourself up enough not to need so much support.

Now, this is not to say that you have to fill every day that you have with different jobs and activities. You may already be only too aware of how important it is for you to have things going on in your life to prevent you from falling too far down emotionally.

Fuelling Yourself

Engaging in some kind of exercise, at least a few times a week, is going to help with your energy levels and it can allow you to experience more positive feelings. Going for a walk, bike ride, or a run might be something that interests you; whereas using weights or body weight exercises might not.

If building up your muscles doesn't interest you, it might be in your best interest to change your outlook. One of the things that you are working towards at this point in time is emotional strength, and if your muscles are weak, it can be a lot harder for you to feel strong.

Two Ways

Thus, if your muscles are strong it can allow you to feel a lot stronger than you would otherwise. The physical strength of your body will have an effect on how you feel emotionally.

Of course, if you feel emotionally weak, it might not matter how physically strong you are. Nevertheless, it is still a good idea for you to make sure that you take good care of your physical self.

The Right Nutrients

Other pieces of the puzzle are eating the right foods and taking the right supplements, these will further enhance your ability to do this work on yourself. You may eat meat or you might not, or you might be a vegan, it doesn't matter.

What matters is that you eat the foods that give you the energy that you need and enable your body to perform at its best. When it comes to supplements, there are a few that can be of benefit to you.

The Basics

Magnesium, omega 3, B vitamins and probiotics can give your body and mind the support that it needs during this time. Magnesium, often described as the master mineral, can help you to relax and to have a deeper sleep.

Omega 3 is essential for your body and brain, with it being something that will benefit you in numerous ways. B vitamins are also good for your wellbeing, in addition to having the ability to improve your energy and memory, amongst other things.

Healthy Gut Healthy Brain

In recent years, it has become increasingly clear how important the gut microbiome is when it comes to physical, mental and emotional health. For many, many years it was thought that it was all about the brain, but recent research has shown that this is not the truth.

35

One example is that it has been said that over ninety percent of serotonin and over fifty percent of dopamine is made in this area. What this illustrates is that if this area of your being is not healthy, it is going to be a further challenge for you to be in a good place.

What You Can Do

Taking a probiotic can help, and this can be from a tablet or by eating unpasteurized sauerkraut, kimchi or kefir. The ideal might be for you to go on a detox program to get your microbiome back in order.

It can all depend on if you have the means to do so, yet if you don't, making a few simple and inexpensive changes can still make a difference. Along with taking probiotics, what will also help is limiting the amount of sugar that you consume.

The Guidance is Available

Sugar is not good for your gut or your brain. You might have to gradually wean yourself off sugar, due to how long you have been having it and how addictive it is.

In each of these areas, it will be best for you to do your own research and to come to your own conclusion about what is and what isn't right for you. Trust that you will be led in the right direction and make the correct decisions.

The Third Part

The Third Part

Healing The Trauma Inside You

If you are in a position where you haven't got the means to work with a therapist or healer, it doesn't mean that there is nothing that you can do. And even if you do have the means to do so, you can still work on yourself in your own time.

When you work with a therapist or healer, there will be the positive regard that you receive and the emotional work that takes place. These two things are a vital part of your healing journey, no doubt about it.

The Other Part

What you may find that you are unable to deal with during this time is the fear, anxiety, panic and even the terror that you may be carrying. Furthermore, there could be times when your body shuts down, thereby stopping you from being aware of your feelings.

If this does happen, it will be clear that you will need another way to resolve what is taking place inside you. And even if you find that your body rarely shuts down and goes numb, you will still need a way to deal with the part of your being that can't be changed by altering your thoughts, behaviour or by crying out unmet childhood needs.

A Different Approach

When you start to resolve this trauma – the fear, anxiety and terror – that is locked inside your body and brain, it will be a lot easier for you to connect to your inner child and to do the emotional work. Once your body loosens up, it can create the space and the strength for

41

your emotional self to express itself, and free up the energy that you need to do this work.

This is something that can take place through using something called Total Release Experience®, or TRE for short. Essentially, this is a physical exercise that will allow you to release your trauma. Your body will twitch, shake, and tremor, which is what animals do to release stress.

A Power Tool

There is a muscle group that connects our upper and lower body known as the psoas, and this muscle – as well as others – contracts when we experience a traumatic event. In this practice, you will learn to initiate your body's innate ability to tremor and hence release held tensions and symptoms of stress and anxiety from trauma.

In order for you to be able to use this technique, you would be advised to undergo the right training and get guidance from an authorised TRE® practitioner. Fortunately, it is relatively inexpensive to learn TRE, and after the second session, you will be able to practice at home.

This is a self-help, self-regulating practice that can save you thousands of pounds while also completely transforming your life. You will be utilising your body's natural ability to heal, and you will gradually become more resilient as time goes by – as long as you practice regularly.

Another Powerful Tool

Another technique that you can use to heal your trauma is something called The Havening Techniques®. This has been described as a method that has been designed to change the brain, so that the

42

memory is de-traumatized and its negative effects are removed from both the psyche and the body.

What is also part of the practice is something called Havening Touch®. This is, ultimately, where the sensory input of human touch is used as a therapeutic tool.

This is something that you can experience with the assistance of a certified Havening Techniques practitioner or by yourself – there are numerous videos online that show you how to do it.

When it comes to whether you work with a certified practitioner or try this by yourself, it can depend on what is going on for you. If you are currently not in a good way, working

Two More Options

Somatic Experiencing is another technique that can help you to heal your trauma, with this being something that is relatively easy to learn. You might prefer this technique, or, you may want to use both.

There is something else that you can use to settle yourself down and this is called Neurofeedback. This can be very powerful; the downside is that it is not cheap and it might not even last.

A Process

If you have the means, it might be a good idea for you to invest in this. Yet if you are not in a good place financially, it will probably be better for you to learn one of the techniques above.

That way you won't spend a lot of money and you will have a way to heal your own trauma. The thing to keep in mind is that your healing journey is a marathon, not a sprint.

The Healing Paradox

If you are in a bad way, you might be happy to throw money at just about everything that promises to assist you. The desire that you have to heal yourself is a good thing, yet it can also create problems for you.

It has been said that we can have anything we want as long as we don't need it. This is why the very act of wanting to heal can prevent it from happening. This is something for you to keep in mind whenever you notice that you are getting impatient.

The Fourth Part

The Fourth Part

Meditation

Another thing that you can do when in your own company, that can help you to relax, to develop your ability to observe what is taking place within you as opposed to getting knocked around by it and can have a positive effect on your brain, is to meditate. This doesn't mean that you will need to sit cross-legged in an empty room for an hour every day.

If this is seen as an obligation, which is possible, if you only follow what works for someone else and don't find what works for you, it will be a lot harder for you to stick to it. This is about you finding something that works for you, not someone else.

Start Small

One thing that you could do is to start off by doing about ten minutes of meditation, a few times a week. During this time you can breathe into your stomach (five seconds in, five seconds out is said to be best for calming the vagus nerve), and focus on your breath and the different sensations of your body.

By doing this, it will take you out of your mind and into the present moment, and allow you to see that you are the observer of your mind, not your mind itself. This will allow you to develop an adult self, too, the part of you that will be there for your inner child.

A Number of Locations

You could meditate in a quiet room or you could go out into nature and spend time in a woodland or a field, for example. Going somewhere like this is likely to be more calming for you than going into a busy area.

Not only won't there be any distractions in nature, but, simply being there can allow you to relax. Listening to relaxing music or a meditation audio might make it even easier for you to do this.

A Gradual Build-Up

After a short time, you may want to meditate for longer than ten minutes and to continue this practice every day. The more you do it the stronger your observer self is likely to become and the better the results are likely to be.

There are many benefits to meditating. These range from sleeping better, having a better memory, feeling more at peace, being less reactive and not getting so easily caught up in drama and negativity. The time and effort that you put into doing this is then going to end up impacting the rest of your life – you will become more aware.

Fear of Abandonment – How To Heal Your Fear of Abandonment

51

The Fifth Part

The Fifth Part

A New Connection

Previously, I wrote that the interpersonal bridge between you and your caregivers didn't form - your connection to the rest of humanity that would have allowed you to feel accepted and as though you belonged - and this is not the only thing that won't have formed. Through not receiving the care that you needed to get your developmental needs met, it would have stopped you from being able to develop a sense of trust in the world, positive expectations and a knowing that you would be supported.

If your needs had been met on a consistent basis during this time, it would have been very different. Your foundations would have been strong.

Two Stages

In the beginning, you would have seen your caregiver/s as being the people who provided you what you needed to survive and as time went by, this would have gradually changed. In addition to the inner strength that you would have developed and the positive expectations that you formed, this time in your life would have given you the knowing that life would support you and provide you with whatever you needed.

Another way of looking at this would be to say that your survival would have been attached to your caregiver/s and as time went by, it ended up being internalised. This can be seen as a natural part of growing up, and becoming an interdependent human being.

Different Sources

You would realise that the money that you need to survive and even thrive would come from other people but that these people are not in control of whether or not you have something. Other people are then just a channel for you to receive what you need.

This would stop you from becoming dependent on them and putting them on a pedestal. For example, if you worked for someone else, you wouldn't see that person as being in control of your survival.

Your Reality

But as your early years were different, it would have meant that you were unable to receive what you needed and then to gradually detach your survival from your caregivers and for this to be something that was internalised. The trauma that is inside you will stop you from being able to accept the truth; the truth that the universe or God, or whatever resonates with you, is there to support you.

As you are a child of the universe or God, it means that you are not separate from anyone or anything. The mind is the only thing that sees everything as being separate, the body is aware of its connection to everything else.

Another Perspective

A different way of looking at this would be to say that while your mother and father were unable to be there for you as a child, what will be there for you now is mother earth and father sky. These two sources will be unconditional in their support and will provide you with what you need.

Spending a short while in nature will reveal how abundant this source is and that there is enough to go around. Surely, this is the type of understanding and connection that indigenous tribes have.

Keeping It Real

At this stage, it doesn't matter if you would describe yourself as spiritual or even religious, what matters is that you do what you need to move forward. So as you heal the layers of trauma that are inside you, you will be able to feel more connected and you may find that you become more spiritual as time goes by.

The other thing that you can do to feel connected is to spend time in nature. Once again, this could be something that takes place a few times a week or more often.

A Deeper Connection

Through spending time in nature, you may find that you start to feel more connected not only to the world but to your own body. What may help is if you take your shoes and socks off while you are there and walk around barefoot.

You might struggle to understand how this would help, yet that's only if you have bought into the illusion, of separation, that your mind creates. If there is nothing on your feet, it will allow your body to actually connect with the earth.

Further Benefits

Spending time in nature can also allow you to develop a sense of security in yourself and to feel more integrated. Providing you go somewhere that is quiet, you will be able to get an idea of what it is like to be calm and this can start to sink in.

Unlike when you are around others, when you are in nature you won't be required to do anything or to be anyone in particular. Being in this environment can then allow you to just be yourself and this can allow the different parts of you being to settle down.

Other Options

Along with spending time in nature, what can help you to develop a connection with your body to re-anchor yourself in there and to feel more connected, is to practice something like Yoga, Tai Chi or Chi Gong. Doing this can bring you back down into your body and it can allow you to release trapped energy.

You might find that you prefer doing one of these things more than the others, and there is no right or wrong option here; the main thing is that you choose one that works for you. By practicing one of these options on a regular basis, you may find that you feel more connected to your body and the earth and less caught up in your mind and this can then allow you to be more aware of how you feel and to be more grounded.

The Sixth Part

The Sixth Part

Inner Child Work

After you have been assisted by a therapist or healer, or even a support group for a short time, and have been performing the trauma work on yourself and started to become stronger, you may find that you are now ready to carry out healing work on yourself. This will be a time when you get in touch with the child parts within yourself and begin to integrate these split-off parts.

One way to find out if you are ready to carry out this work on yourself is to see if you can actually be there for your child self or whatever child part arises, without merging with it completely. In the same way that a parent would be with their child who is in pain, you may be able to stay in the present and be with this part of you.

Being, Not Doing

When you are in touch with this part of yourself, there will be no need for you to do anything. This means that you won't need to change or fix anything, you will be there for this child with your presence and unconditional love.

You will be surrendering to what is taking place and embracing the feminine element that is inside you. The masculine element, on the other hand, relates to the doing, and while this is needed when it comes to changing your thoughts or beliefs, for instance, it is not needed here.

One Step Back

However, to get to this point will have taken a lot of courage. You will have most likely needed to have worked through a number of different defences to get in contact with what is taking place for you at a deeper level.

This would have been a time when you needed the power of your masculine element; without this, you probably wouldn't have been able to get to this point. For that reason, it wouldn't be right for me to say that this part of you has no part to play here.

Be Patient

This element will have enabled you to get to this point and it will be needed as you go even deeper inside yourself. Once you have got in touch with this part of yourself, it may take you a little while to build its trust.

Unsurprisingly, this part of you may find it hard to trust anyone and so you will need to prove to it that you won't harm it in any way. One way to get an idea of what it is like for this part of you would be to imagine what it would be like for a small animal to trust you; like this animal, your inner child will be in a very vulnerable position.

A Dialogue

By not judging this part of yourself or trying to change it in any way, it will start to feel safe enough to open up to you. It can start to tell you how it feels and it can tell you about what it wants to say to certain people.

There are likely to be times when you end up crying out the pain that this part of you wasn't able to cry out many, many years ago. Crying is a vital part of inner child work, so do what you can to surrender when this takes place.

A Limiting Belief

If you find that whenever you cry you try to stop yourself and even feel bad, it will be a good idea for you to look into why this is. It could show that you have a number of erroneous beliefs about crying.

You may find that you believe that crying is a sign of weakness. In reality, it takes strength to cry and crying is an excellent way for you to let go of the emotional baggage that is inside you.

An Altered State of consciousness

When you are in contact with your inner child, you will be in touch with your unconscious mind. This is why the work that you do with this part of you will have such a big effect on your life.

If you were to have hypnotherapy, for instance, you are likely to go to the same level that this inner child operates on. Thus, if you ever find that it is hard for you to connect to this part of yourself; you can listen to an audio that will guide you to this level.

Other Ways

What you could also do to get in touch with this part of yourself is to look at old pictures of when you were a child. Looking at these pictures may end up triggering something inside you, thereby allowing you to work through whatever arises.

Another option would be for you to put your hands on the parts of your body where you feel tension as this can allow you to connect to the pain that is inside you. If you don't use your hands in this way, you may find that it is hard for you to connect to how you feel, at least in the beginning.

65

Additional Support

What can also help you with this is if you learn Reiki healing. Not only can this assist with your healing, it can make it easier for you to connect with the pain that is inside your body.

With the heat from your hands you can warm up areas of your body that are cold or unresponsive and to move the energy that is stuck inside you. At the right time, this is something that you can learn online for a reasonable price.

Plenty to Say

The more pain that you work through and the stronger your connection is with this part of yourself, the easier it will be for you to do this work. What will also play a part here is that once you inner child realises that it can trust you, it will be more likely to reach out to you.

This part of you can feel the need to say things to your mother and father, and any siblings or other family members that were around at this stage in your life. Your mother or father can then appear in your inner world and your inner child can express what it was unable to say all those years ago.

Changing The Past

What happened in the past can't be changed, that much is clear, but that doesn't mean that you can't change the experience that your inner child had during this time. Through your presence, your inner child can feel safe enough to express feelings and say things that it didn't feel safe enough to reveal previously.

Your mother or father who appears in your inner world can then end up apologising for what took place. One way to see this process would be to say that your inner child will be talking to your mother and father's higher self, the part of them that is far more evolved than the version that actually existed.

It Can't Be Rushed

The ideal might be for you to undertake this work for a few weeks or even a few months and then you are finished, but this is not how it works. For one thing, there are many layers of pain inside you and each layer of pain will typically appear when you are ready to work through it, not before.

In a way, each layer is like another weight that you would add to a bar at the gym; each weight has to be added over a period of time or else you would be wiped out. Similarly, as you work through each layer your being will get stronger and this will prepare you for the next layer that arises.

The Outcome

Your emotional body will change as will your brain, and you will become a more integrated and whole human being during the process. There will be less conflict within you, making it easier for you to feel at peace, to listen to and express your true self, and to stand your ground when you need to.

And by being there for this part of yourself and giving it what it didn't receive from its caregivers, you will need less from others. You will start to get a clearer idea of what needs other people can meet and what needs they can't meet, and if you actually want something or if it is something your inner child wants.

The Seventh Part

The Seventh Part

The Importance of Human Connection

What may be clear to you at this point is that in order for you to heal, you need the support of others; not all the time but some of the time. There are things you can do by yourself and things that you can't.

It has been said that it takes a village to raise a child, and it could be said that it takes a small team to heal a person. This can be the healer or therapist that you work with, and you can end up working with a number of different people as time goes by, and there can also be the people in your life who are there for you.

Quality over Quantity

Having a handful of people in your life that you trust and can be yourself with is going to be far better than having numerous people in your life who you don't trust and who you can't be yourself around. The former will greatly enrich your life, while the latter will simply undermine you.

Nonetheless, due to what is currently taking place inside you, you may find that you are not surrounded by the right people. Perhaps there are people in your life who are toxic or maybe you just have people in your life who are not on 'the healing path' and don't understand what you are going through.

This Too shall pass

One way for you to look at what is currently taking place in this area of your life is to simply see it as a stage. The people in your life reflect how you have been in the past and as you change, the people in your life will also change or they will disappear.

71

If you do have people in your life that are toxic, this is naturally going to make it harder for you to grow. Part of you may fear moving on, even though they are not good for you, but when you let go of people like this, it will create the space for the right people to enter your life.

A Number of options

When it comes to where you can meet people who are also on the path, there are a number of different places. There are numerous support groups where you will be able to meet like-minded people.

What you could also do is enrol in different self-help courses or classes, and you may even find that some of these are free. The time and effort that you put in by going to these can pay off in a big way.

Opening Up

Once you have a number of people in your life that you can be yourself with, it will be a lot easier for you to move forward. Instead of hiding who you are and playing a role, you will be able to open up about what is happening in your life.

This is going to help when it comes to letting go of toxic shame and any beliefs that you have that help to keep this feeling in place. Or to be more precise, any beliefs that keep the feeling that may have permeated your whole being in place.

It's Ok

As you know that these people won't judge you and are understanding, you will be able to share your toxic shame with these people. Bringing it out into the open is what will allow it to slowly dissipate and to no longer have such a huge impact on your life.

If this toxic shame was to stay inside you, this wouldn't take place; it would then continue to control how you behave. This is what will happen if you are around people that you can't open up to.

We Are All On Our Own Path

When it comes to the people in your life who are not toxic but who are not on the path, you may find that they start to change through spending time with you. This will mean that you can grow together.

Conversely, you may find that they are not willing to change even if they are open to your conversations. This can be hard to accept especially if you have known each other for a long time, yet it will be important to remember that you can't change anyone.

Focus On Yourself

You can be an example to others but you can't make them change; if you try to do this, you will be violating another person's boundaries and you will be wasting your precious time and energy. If you do have the need to change others, you could take a step back and look into why this is.

It will be far better for you to direct your time and energy into things that you do have control over. And right now, you need to direct a lot of your energy into your own healing.

The Eighth Part

The Eighth Part

Getting In Touch With Your Inherent Worth

If you hadn't previously realised that the toxic shame inside you is one of the main reasons why you find it hard to feel good about yourself, it might be clearer at this point. When you experience toxic shame, you may find that your face feels really hot and that you feel the need to hide yourself away from everyone and everything.

Considering how powerful this is and the nature of it, it is unlikely that positive thoughts and affirmations will do much to change how you feel about yourself. If anything, these things will simply cause you to cover up how you truly feel and to live in denial.

Built On Sand

Taking this approach could result in you building up a false self; a self that is not built on anything substantial. You will then rise up, artificially, and then someone could say or do something and you could come crashing back down to earth.

Your true feelings will have been pushed down, waiting for the time when they could be set free. The external trigger will have just brought up to the surface what was already within you, meaning that how you feel would have had very little to do with what actually took place.

Another Approach

The key will be for you to work through the toxic shame that is inside you and to question what you believe. As this toxic shame leaves your being, it will be a lot easier for you to accept positive messages.

It will take longer for you to feel good about yourself by taking this route but at least you will be building strong foundations. It will be a case of short-term gain, long-term pain, or short-term pain, long-term gain.

What You Can Do

This doesn't mean that you shouldn't use affirmations or do what you can to have positive thoughts though, what it comes down to is that these alone probably won't transform how you feel about yourself. It can be seen as being aware of what these tools can do, and what they can't do – being realistic.

To use an analogy: a hammer wouldn't be used to cut a tree down and a saw wouldn't be used to bang a nail into something. It is not that these tools are no good; it is just that there is a time and a place to use them.

Keep Your Mind Focused

One thing you can do, and this doesn't involve denying how you truly feel, is to make a list of your good traits and the things that you are good at. Initially, due to how you feel and the beliefs that you have, it may be hard for you to recognise these things.

However, by making a list of both of these things, you will be able to see the truth, not the lies that you have come to believe. After you have created this list, you could put it somewhere prominent within easy vision.

The Ninth Part

The Ninth Part

Integrating Your Aggression

If you have spent most of your life trying to please others, a lot of anger may have built up inside you. As you have rarely felt safe enough to listen to your own needs and feelings, even if you have been aware of them, this is to be expected.

Due to what you believe would take place if you were to do this, asserting yourself will be seen as something that is a threat to your very survival. Along with the anger and even rage that you carry from your adult years will most likely be the anger and rage that you carry from your early years.

Your Only Choice

What takes place now that you are an adult will be nothing more than a continuation of what took place when you were a child. Your mind will perceive life in the same way even though it is not the same.

You may have even come to believe that it is wrong for you to get angry and that it is best for you to continue to deny this part of your nature. So if you don't experience fear when you get angry, you could end up feeling guilty and ashamed.

It's Neutral

Ultimately, anger (or rage) is neither good nor bad; it is simply there to notify you that you are being violated or compromised, or that a wound from your past has been triggered. If you are able to listen to this part of you and to utilise the information that it provides, your life is likely to improve.

83

For example, if you get angry and look into why this is and then take the appropriate action, this anger will have assisted you. If, on the other hand, you ignore your anger or allow it to control you, it won't have assisted you.

An Asset

The way for you to embrace this part of your being will be to integrate your aggression; the part of you that is often seen as being 'lower' or even primitive. This is the part of you that gives you energy and allows you to feel alive, to know when your boundaries are being crossed, the strength to assert yourself, and to defend yourself if you are attacked.

When this part of you is integrated with the rest of you, there will be less need for you to get angry. The reason for this is that you will instantly know when something isn't right and take the right action as opposed to tolerating something that isn't right and then getting angry afterwards.

An Important Process

Due to what it was like for you as a child, you wouldn't have consciously chosen to disconnect from your aggression; it would have just happened. There will be a number of things that you can do to gradually embrace this incredibly important part of your being.

Firstly, it will be essential for you to question the beliefs that you have formed when it comes to your anger and aggression, to see if the beliefs serve your highest good. Secondly, working through the emotional pain inside you will allow you to slowly resolve your anger and rage, causing this part of you to settle down.

Deep Pain

Underneath this anger and rage are likely to be a lot of feelings that have a very different energy. Anger and rage can allow you to feel strong and powerful; the other feelings can make you feel very different.

When you go under these two feelings, you may find that you feel incredibly vulnerable. At this level, you can feel helpless, powerless and experience a lot of fear.

Inner Safety

Thirdly, resolving the trauma that is inside you will allow you to feel safe in your own body, which will allow you to embrace this part of your being. Once this inner sense of safety is there, there will be no need for you to deny this part of your being.

Another option for you to get some of your anger and rage out would be to acquire a punching bag and to hit and push it whenever you feel the call to do so. Conversely, you could join a martial arts or boxing class.

The Tenth Part

The Tenth Part

Journaling

Something else that can greatly assist you on your healing journey is a journal. This can be somewhere where you write about whatever is taking place in your mind, body and life – there are no restrictions or limits to this.

You won't need to worry about how it sounds, what other people think or if what you are writing makes any sense. So whatever is taking place inside you, you can simply get it down on paper.

Clarity

If you keep everything within you, what you may find is that it is harder for you to make sense of what is going on. Your mind will be full, making it difficult for new insights to come into your mind.

By using a journal, you will create space for new information to enter your mind. One way to look at this would be to say that the conscious mind is like the desktop of a computer, it can only hold onto so many items.

A New Perspective

Another thing that can happen, after you have written something down, and you have read what you have written, is that you become aware of, or see something, you haven't seen before. It won't have taken a lot of effort for you to write something down, yet you will have been able to gain new insights.

It will be as if you are looking at something from a different angle, allowing you to see it differently. Before you would have only had one part of the picture and now you will have another part or even the whole picture.

Measuring Your Progress

Writing about the steps that you have taken and what has happened can allow you to see that you are advancing. Each step that you take may seem insignificant but over time, each step will add up.

Over time, you will then be able to look back on where you have come from and see that you have come a long way. Yet, if you hadn't taken the time to write about what has been going on for you, it would be a lot harder for you to see this.

Your Choice

There may be times when you write in your journal frequently and there may be times when you don't use it very often. Listen to yourself and go with what works for you; there is no right or wrong way of doing this.

When it comes to what you should do with a journal after you have completely filled it, you may find that you want to keep it for a little while. Alternatively, you may feel the need to burn it so that the energy within it doesn't affect your life – if you would like to find out more about how your possessions affect you, you can look into Feng Shui.

Afterword

Now that you have completed this book, I hope that you have a clearer idea about what you need to do to gradually change your life and that you soon start to get the ball rolling, if you haven't already. What matters is that you keep going and don't give up on yourself.

If there are times when you do give up and are unable to keep going, try to be kind to yourself. You may find that although you are able to be compassionate to others, it is hard for you to be compassionate towards yourself.

One thing that you can do to be more compassionate towards yourself is to imagine how you would respond to a small child who has made a mistake. Would you judge this child and put them down? Of course you wouldn't.

How you would treat this child is exactly the way in which you deserve to be treated when you make a mistake or do something that doesn't serve you. Another thing you can do to connect to this type of energy is to imagine how a supportive friend, teacher or someone else who has supported you in life, would respond to you in a situation like this.

Once you are able to be compassionate to yourself, and this will get a lot easier as you heal your inner wounds, it will take less effort for you to rise up again and to move on from a setback. The important thing will be for you to remember that in each moment of your life, you are doing your best.

You are not perfect, you are not supposed to be; if anything, you are perfectly imperfect. It takes courage to do this work and this is something that you can bring to mind if ever you feel a bit deflated.

The easy option would be for you to simply tolerate how your life is and not to do anything about it. You are not prepared to do this, so do what you can to focus on this fact and think about the progress that you are making, however small it may seem.

Also, what I have laid out in this book is based upon what I have learnt until this point in time. What this means is that it is not the only way to work through this issue.

So stay curious and leave your mind open to any information that will come your way, both internally and externally. In other words, trust your inner guidance and you will know what you need to know and when you need to know it.

If there is anything that you would like to share with me or if you have any questions, please get in touch.

I wish you the very best on your journey.

Oliver JR Cooper

Acknowledgements

At the beginning of 2015, I wrote a book called 'Abandonment: Is The Fear Of Abandonment Controlling Your Life?' At this point in time I thought that I had a handle on it, how wrong I was.

If I hadn't learnt anything else about this, and had more to say, I certainly wouldn't have put this book together. So since that stage in my life, I have been very fortunate to have been assisted by a number of different people.

One of those people is Ben Ralston. It is perfectly clear that my life would be very different if our paths hadn't crossed.

There is also Caroline Purvey, who taught me TRE. I feel very grateful that I came into contact with her.

Some of the other people who have assisted me are no longer alive, but who assisted me through the work that they left behind. Three of these people are Arthur Janov, Anthony Storr and R.D. Laing.

Crossing paths again with Errol Campbell, a healer who worked with my father, and doing a number of live video calls was also a massive help. During this time, I was reminded of how important inner child work is.

At the end of the day, I wouldn't be where I am now if it wasn't for these people. Of course, I have played my part, but that doesn't negate the part that other people have played.

Made in the USA
Las Vegas, NV
10 December 2024

13848903R00061